How to Be an AZTEC WARRIOR

by Nel Yomtov

PEBBLE
a capstone imprint

Pebble is published by Capstone,
1710 Roe Crest Drive, North Mankato, Minnesota 56003
capstonepub.com

Copyright © 2026 by Capstone. All rights reserved. No part of this publication may be reproduced in whole or in part, or stored in a retrieval system, or transmitted in any form or by any means, electronic, mechanical, photocopying, recording, or otherwise, without written permission of the publisher.

Library of Congress Cataloging-in-Publication Data is available on the Library of Congress website.

ISBN: 9798875226816 (hardcover)
ISBN: 9798875234644 (paperback)
ISBN: 9798875234651 (ebook PDF)

Summary: Journey back in time to an ancient civilization and become an Aztec warrior.

Editorial Credits
Editor: Alison Deering; Designer: Bobbie Nuytten; Media Researcher: Svetlana Zhurkin; Production Specialist: Whitney Schaefer

Image Credits
Alamy: Dorling Kindersley ltd, 20, The Picture Art Collection, 19; Bridgeman Images: 13, 23, 27, © Bodleian Libraries, University of Oxford, 8, 9, Peter Newark American Pictures, 10; Getty Images: Christine_Kohler, 29, Dorling Kindersley, 5, 12, 17, FairytaleDesign, 15, Grafissimo, 18, kostins, 26; The Metropolitan Museum of Art: Museum Purchase, 1900, 16; Shutterstock: adolf martinez soler (stone wall), cover and throughout, Burak Erdal, cover (bottom), JosueViquez, cover (top), Yip Po Yu (texture), cover and throughout; SuperStock: DeAgostini, 11, 21, 25, The Art Archive/Picture Desk, 7

Any additional websites and resources referenced in this book are not maintained, authorized, or sponsored by Capstone. All product and company names are trademarks™ or registered® trademarks of their respective holders.

Table of Contents

Introduction
Warriors of the Aztec Empire 4

Chapter 1
Born to Be a Warrior 6

Chapter 2
Tools of the Trade 14

Chapter 3
Days of Peace 20

Chapter 4
Attack! 24

Test Your Aztec Knowledge 30
Glossary 31
Index 32
About the Author 32

Words in **bold** are in the glossary.

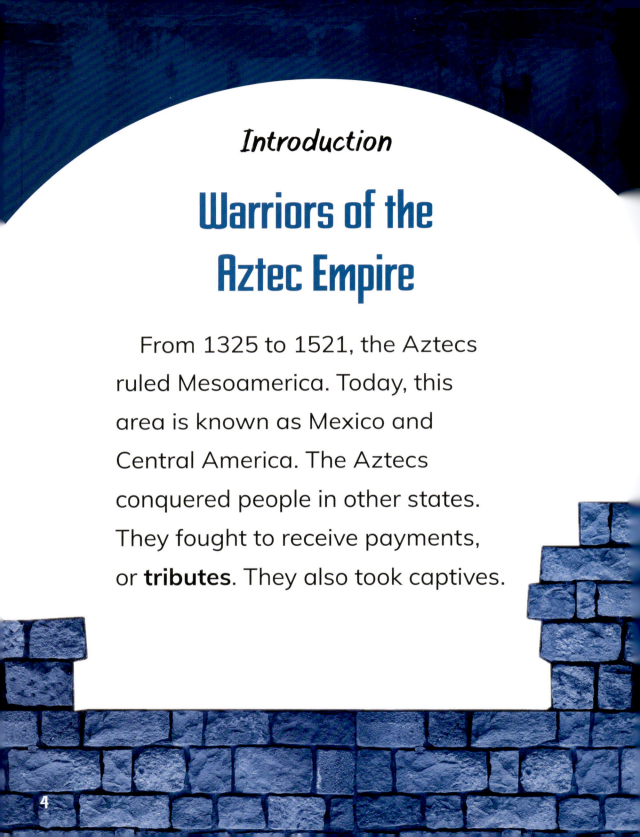

Introduction

Warriors of the Aztec Empire

From 1325 to 1521, the Aztecs ruled Mesoamerica. Today, this area is known as Mexico and Central America. The Aztecs conquered people in other states. They fought to receive payments, or **tributes**. They also took captives.

Aztec warriors were a key part of building and expanding the empire. They were respected and honored for their fighting skills and bravery. Kings rewarded successful warriors with gifts of land, clothing, and jewelry.

Do YOU have what it takes to be an Aztec warrior?

Chapter 1

Born to Be a Warrior

You are born into a commoner family. You have no rank or title. Your father is a farmer. From the ages of 3 to 15, you live with your parents.

If you are a boy, you help work on your family's small farm. If you are a girl, you learn how to cook and keep the house in order.

Your farm chores make you stronger with each passing year. You carry wood, water, and supplies. You do other heavy work in the fields such as plowing, planting, and harvesting.

At age 15, you decide to attend the House of Youth. Here you will be trained for warfare. The school is not for everyone. Other friends your age may decide to remain farmers.

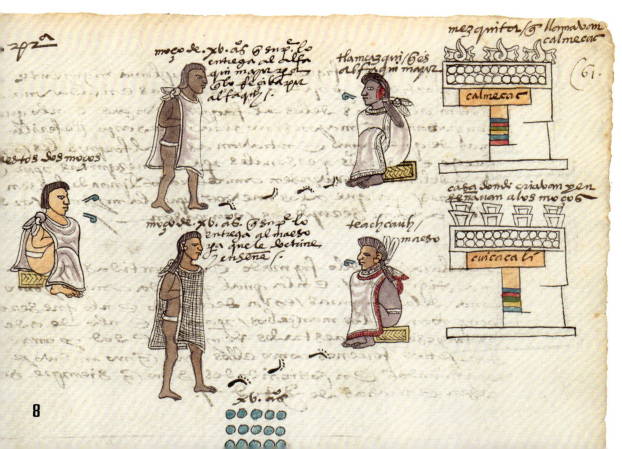

Boys from noble families attend a different school. They are trained as priests and leaders in the military. But fear not. You can still become an honored member of society by capturing enemies in battle.

Training at the House of Youth leaves little time for **academic** or religious studies. You play traditional Aztec ball games. They help build **endurance** and agility. You'll need these qualities on the battlefield.

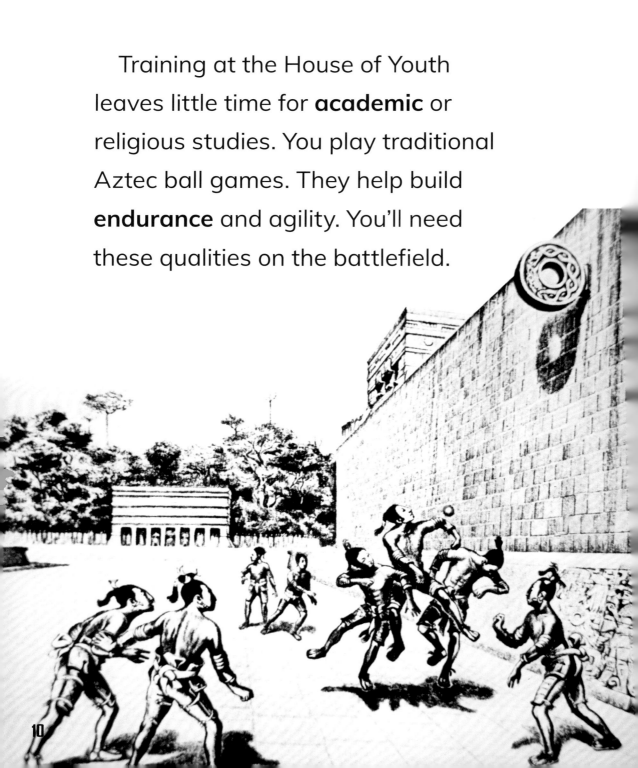

You also participate in pretend battles with other students. You compete for food and gifts. Older warriors teach you how to use Aztec weapons. These include bows and arrows, **slings**, clubs, and spears.

If you show great promise, you will move on to training with a sword and shield. Your goal is to become an Eagle or Jaguar warrior. These are the highest levels of Aztec fighters open to commoners. To do so, you will have to capture at least four enemies in battle.

By age 20, your training is complete. You have proven yourself capable of fighting in the Aztec army!

Warrior Tip #1: Use Your Feet!

Improve your fighting skills by dancing! Dancing will help you practice foot movements and build strength and speed.

Chapter 2
Tools of the Trade

Your main weapon is a **macuahuitl**. It is a type of wooden club. Very sharp **obsidian** blades are attached to its edges. This hard, glass-like stone is formed from cooling **lava**. It is many times sharper than today's sharpest steel blade.

A one-handed form of the weapon is about 3 feet (91 centimeters) long. This shorter version is used in close combat. The two-handed version could be as tall as an adult man!

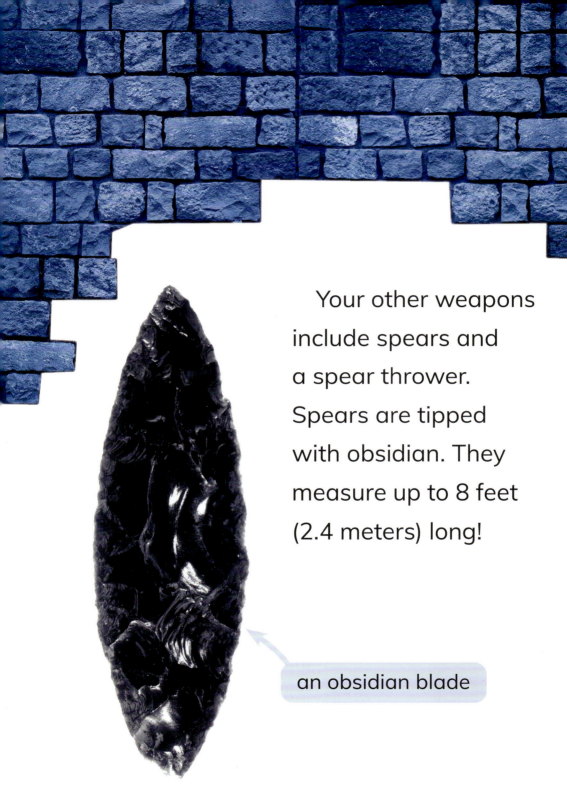

Your other weapons include spears and a spear thrower. Spears are tipped with obsidian. They measure up to 8 feet (2.4 meters) long!

an obsidian blade

The spear thrower is a tool that measures between 5 and 24 inches (13 and 61 cm) long. It has a hook at one end. The hook fits into a notch on the end of a spear shaft. You whip the thrower forward as if throwing a baseball. This sends the spear on its deadly path.

spear thrower

In combat, you carry a round shield made from **cane** or bamboo. You also wear a battle suit and helmet. Your battle suit includes a padded pullover shirt. It is worn under a full-length bodysuit also made of cotton. The suit is lightweight and allows you to move freely.

Warrior Tip #2: Be a Metal Head!

Be a clever Aztec warrior! Cover your shield in copper for the best protection.

On your head you wear a simple cone-shaped helmet. It is made of **mahogany**. If you perform well in battle, your leaders will reward you with a colorfully painted helmet. It will be carved to look like a jaguar, coyote, or other animal.

Chapter 3

Days of Peace

Ball games are an important form of entertainment and sport for your people. You play these games as you rise through the military ranks. They are practice for the battlefield. Many nobles come to watch. You win trophies for your performance on the ball court.

Religion also plays an important role in your daily life. You attend services and festivals that honor the Aztec gods.

Though you are a successful warrior, you still have daily chores. You farm corn, beans, and other foods with your family. In your spare time, you may make pottery or objects of gold or silver. You also make cutting stones from obsidian. Other warriors hire you to make their weapons.

You enjoy these peaceful days, but you are trained to be a warrior. Are you prepared to fight at a moment's notice?

Chapter 4

Attack!

Your leader orders an attack on a **rival** state. It lies about 150 miles (241 kilometers) from your village. You and an army of nearly 75,000 warriors will travel on foot to reach the enemy.

You cross hot, dry deserts and pass through humid, tropical rainforests. In a basket, you take **tortillas**, beans, fruits, vegetables, dried deer meat, and more.

These items will be your food on the long march. You will refill your supplies from previously captured kingdoms along the way.

You march for many days. Finally, you reach your destination. A huge army stands guard in front of the city's walls. They are ready for your attack!

Warrior Tip #3: Earn a Noble Honor

Carrying flowers was a privilege normally granted only to the nobles. Perform well on the battlefield, and your leaders will grant you this special honor.

The battle begins. Both sides fire arrows and hurl spears and stones at one another. The two armies recover from the attack and rush forward into battle.

You slash at your enemy with your weapon. You want to disarm him and knock him down. Then, two Aztec youths will rush forward. They will tie him up as a prisoner.

If you succeed, this will be the fourth enemy you've captured. You'll become a Jaguar or Eagle warrior.

The enemy lunges at you with his spear. You quickly step aside and raise your shield to knock him down. Will this be your fourth capture? Or will today's battle be your last?

Test Your Aztec Knowledge

1. What is a macuahuitl?
    a. a club-like Aztec weapon
    b. a Mesoamerican food
    c. a type of helmet worn by Aztec warriors

2. The area of Mesoamerica includes:
    a. Mexico and South America
    b. South America and the islands of the Caribbean Sea
    c. Mexico and Central America

3. What is the House of Youth?
    a. a school for Aztec warrior training
    b. a sports training camp
    c. a place of higher learning for Aztec nobility

4. The sharp stone used to make Aztec weapons is called:
    a. quartz
    b. obsidian
    c. limestone

5. What is tribute?
    a. a river that flows into a larger river
    b. a form of Aztec government
    c. payments made by conquered states to another state

Answers: 1) a, 2) c, 3) a, 4) b, 5) c

If you answered all the questions correctly, the job of Aztec warrior is yours! If not, take another read through this book and try the test again!

Glossary

academic (ak-uh-DEM-ik)—having to do with study and learning

cane (KAYN)—a plant or grass with a woody, sometimes hollow stem

endurance (en-DUR-enss)—the ability to do something difficult for a long time

lava (LAH-vuh)—the hot, liquid rock that pours out of a volcano when it erupts

macuahuitl (mahk-wah-WEE-tul)—a club-like weapon with obsidian blades used by Aztec warriors

mahogany (muh-HOG-uh-nee)—a type of reddish-brown wood

obsidian (uhb-SID-ee-uhn)—a dark, glass-like rock formed by cooling volcanic lava

rival (RYE-vuhl)—someone with whom you compete

sling (SLING)—a strap or loop of leather used for throwing stones

tortilla (tor-TEE-yuh)—a flat, round bread made from corn or flour

tribute (TRIB-yoot)—a payment demanded by someone with power, like a ruler or state

Index

ages, 6, 8, 13

ball games, 10, 20

captives, 4, 9, 12, 28

chores, 7, 22

clothing, 18

farming, 6–7, 8, 22

food, 24–25

helmets, 18, 19

House of Youth, 8, 10

Mesoamerica, 4

nobility, 9, 20, 26

obsidian, 14, 16, 22

rankings, 12, 28

religion, 21

shields, 18

training, 8, 9, 10, 11, 12, 13

tributes, 4

weapons, 11, 12, 14, 16–17, 22, 27

About the Author

Nel Yomtov is an award-winning author of children's nonfiction books and graphic novels. He specializes in writing about history, current events, biography, architecture, and military history. He has written numerous graphic novels for Capstone, including the recent *The Wright Brothers Take Flight*, *The Christmas Truce of World War I*, and *D-Day Training Turned Deadly: The Exercise Tiger Disaster*. In 2020 he self-published *Baseball 100*, an illustrated book featuring the 100 greatest players in baseball history. Nel lives in the New York City area.